Praise for Antonia Fraser

Must You Go?: My Life with Harold Pinter

"Combining disarming emotional frankness with restrained elegance, Antonia Fraser weaves her diary entries and memories into a compelling and moving history of a long, passionate relationship."

Katie Owen, *Sunday Times*

"[Written] with exemplary clarity and courage...Fraser keeps her gaze steady and her heart open."

Boyd Tonkin, *Independent*

"This book – full of funny and tender things – satisfies on more than one level. It is an intimate account of the life and habits of a major artist; it is a pencil sketch of British high society in the second half of the twentieth century; and it is, more than either of these things, and much more unusually, a wonderfully full description of the deep pleasures and comforts of married love."

Sam Leith, *Spectator*

"Unremittingly delicious: strange, rarefied, frequently hilarious." Rachel Cooke, *Observer*

"It takes a daring biographer to turn her sharp eye on her own life as Antonia Fraser does so movingly and beautifully in her memoir."
Tina Brown, *Daily Beast*

My History: A Memoir of Growing Up

"*My History*, a captivating memoir of her childhood and early youth…is a delight from start to finish. Antonia Fraser is warm, amusing, intelligent, generous and original. She says that her idea of perfect happiness is to be alone in a room with a house full of people. I can't think of a better way to start the year than to be alone in a room with this book."
Cressida Connolly, *Spectator*

"*My History* is a hugely enjoyable squishy romp, the literary equivalent of a big crumbling meringue at a society wedding."
Roger Lewis, *The Times*

Our Israeli Diary

Also by Antonia Fraser

Historical Works

Our Israeli Diary

Of That Time, Of That Place
8–22 May 1978

ANTONIA FRASER

ONEWORLD

A Oneworld Book

First published by Oneworld Publications, 2017

ISBN 978-1-78607-153-8

Printed and bound in Great Britain by
Clays Ltd, St Ives plc

Oneworld Publications
10 Bloomsbury Street
London WC1B 3SR
England

Dedicated to Harold's parents,
Frances Pinter, 1904–1992, and Jack Pinter,
1902–1997, who loved Israel.

Contents

List of Illustrations

The Cableway (courtesy of Berthold Werner/ Wikimedia Commons)

Masada

Harold's certificate commemorating his ascent to the summit of Masada

The guest house in Jerusalem where Antonia and Harold stayed (courtesy of Rafael Ben-Ari/ Alamy Stock Photo)

Via Dolorosa in 1978 (courtesy of Tony Spina/ the Walter P. Reuther Library, Wayne State University)

Conductor Zubin Mehta (courtesy of Getty Images/Bettmann)

Cellist and conductor Mstislav Rostropovich (courtesy of Benoit Gysembergh/*Paris Match* via Getty Images)

Jackie Kennedy Onassis (courtesy of Ron Galella/WireImage via Getty Images)

Shimon Peres in 1978 (courtesy of Keystone Pictures USA/Alamy Stock Photo)

Peter Halban and Antonia

Harold and Antonia with Harold's parents, Frances and Jack Pinter

A Note on the Text

This is an immediate record of our stay in Israel in May 1978. I wrote it every morning on my little portable typewriter while Harold had his shower. At this point Harold and I had been living together since August 1975 but were not yet able to get married. He was 47 and I was 45. We were finally married in November 1980.

I first re-read the diary nearly 40 years later, in May 2016, when I came across it by chance clearing out an old cupboard. Writing my memoir of my life with Harold, *Must You Go?*, I relied on memory and the narrative captions round the prints in my photograph album.

Israel in 1978

May marked the thirtieth anniversary of the founding of the State of Israel, in 1948.

Menachem Begin, founder of the Likud Party, had become Prime Minister of Israel when his party won the election in 1977.

Moshe Dayan, military commander and politician, had been Defence Minister during the Six Day War of 1967.

Golda Meir had been Prime Minister of Israel from 1969 and resigned in the aftermath of the Yom Kippur War of 1973.

Shimon Peres was first elected to the Knesset, the Israeli parliament, in 1959. Later, as leader of the Labour Party, he would become Prime Minister of Israel in a National Unity Government in 1984, and in 2007 President. He died in September 2016.

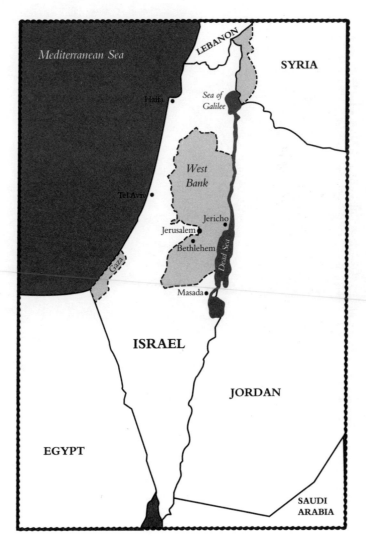

Israel in 1978

We get down to the cable-car. In the car H, sweating heavily and
looking extremely ill, still no spectacles, staggers onto the solitary
bench. It is occupied by another, heavy-set, man who begins:
"As an Irish-American, may I salute a fellow Britisher?" It would
only happen to H.... In the end Peter and I turn round and forcibly
shut him up. "Why is he ill or something?" queries the man in a baffled
and rather hurt but still very grating voice.
So we are down.
H later: You know I told you I didn't know what the next stage of
vertigo was. Well now I know. Coldness. Nausea.
Me: You were a hero - you got down. With your hand.
He gives me a copy of Yadim's splendid <u>Masada</u> inscribed "to Antonia,
the girl who got me down alive".

From the original diary…

Monday 8 May

Writing this sitting in the aeroplane (already delayed one hour for lack of incoming aircraft and now for traffic congestion about another hour). We are off to Israel. Neither of us have ever been before, neither of us for want of asking. H. must have been invited many times and in my previous life I nearly went three times with my husband Hugh, a pro-Israel Tory MP, who also received many invitations. I was often prevented by chances which now seem premonitions. Harold has concentrated his shopping for the trip on *shoes*, many pairs of bi-coloured leather and canvas shoes which I hope mean he intends to go sight-seeing. I have bought a sand-coloured skirt from St. Laurent and a white blouse from M & S (loyalty) and *also* some shoes. Our feet seem to have been much on our minds. I think we both believe we shall tramp through a great deal of history.

Harold, rather providently, has also thought of his eyes. He has ordered/bought a new pair of prescription sunglasses, abnormally huge and rather sinister. Perhaps he sees them as protective?

A typical flight to Israel in 1978 (we are first class, but it really doesn't affect the issue) involves the following procedures:

1) You re-collect your luggage from the check-in, labelled also with your name unlike most flights, and wheel it yourself to a gateway marked S.

H.: "Note that all other countries in the world have a shared gateway. One country has one gateway."

We queue there for perhaps 30 minutes. In the queue some Sieffs.

I have caught my breath at the sight of Teddy Sieff, the survivor of the assassin's bullet fired by Carlos the Jackal.

Me: "You're not supposed to get on a flight containing a prominent Jew, and here's that hero Teddy Sieff."

I am glad to see that Teddy at least is guided through, tho' later he complains about this, quite genuinely:

T.S.: "You see, unlike you, I have come to believe in a classless society."

I do not contradict this, as in the first class lounge H. and I have had one of our ridiculous summer-lightning rows about the presence of the C.I.A. in Angola (!!!) so I am wary of contradicting anyone…

Well, as I was saying,

2) A very thorough search of your main luggage. But we had a Scotsman – Aberdeen – who asked for my autograph at the end of it. This propensity of the British for adapting and making pleasant what must be endured.

The girl who,

3) searched our hand-luggage also ventured the view: "I wish I was going with you. Perhaps one day" instead of just coldly hating us all.

Incidentally. Me to H.: "That customs man, like Mr. Goldenberg at the Carlyle Hotel, was not your fan…" Shortly afterwards the customs man reappeared, panting, and asked for H.'s autograph.

5

How wrong I was. I liked the man's approach to his endless and tiresome job, creating a unique autograph book. "I have searched the luggage of…"

4) We hear the flight is delayed. A low moment. H. gets a beer. I disappear to the Ladies, being disabled by my wretched skin allergy, the alleged poison ivy. When I return, H. has some champagne and we both feel better.

5) To the first class lounge where Teddy's wife Lois is very excitable and sweet about Mishkenot Sha'ananim, the artists' colony where we are going to stay. Later Teddy himself, a handsome and rather fit 70-year-old (who would ever have guessed?), talks to us of his Anglo-Saxon Kibbutz 3 at Tiberias.

6) A long queue for boarding, with another quite detailed search.

And now we are here sitting…

And now about to take off.

Preparation: I've read Saul Bellow's book about Israel, and am reading the former Foreign Minister Abba Eban's autobiography which gives an extraordinary picture of the 1947 negotiations. I've bought *O Jerusalem!* by Larry Collins and Dominique Lapierre and a book by Moshe Dayan. I haven't read so much Jewish history since I was working on my biography of Oliver Cromwell in the 1970s: his desire for the readmission of the Jews to England.

H., I sense, is just *thinking*…

The actual arrival at Tel Aviv airport, after all this, was smooth. A large lounge for collecting luggage. Rather less chaos than at Heathrow. A taxi came from Mishkenot. We made a journey of about an hour through the night. Sights: a prison – clearly so – was lit up with fairy lights, a huge red and white star of David for Independence. With its barbed wire and searchlights it nevertheless looked odd to have this particular celebratory star…

Impossible to sense the countryside tho' reminded of Teddy Sieff saying it had all been
desert when he first came.

H.: "We should not take this road for granted."

All the same, everything modern and therefore
unremarkable, even the hilly lights of Jerusalem,
even the new town itself, until we suddenly
came on the famous historic windmill, well lit-
up, *then* Mishkenot built into the hill, and above
us, also lightly illuminated, a long (very clean)
castle wall.

The first sense that we were actually in
Jerusalem, although the lightness of the stone
still made it seem unreal.

Annie, the den mother of Mishkenot, greeted
us: a particularly kind of bright even merry look
which already I associate with Israeli women on
the strength of the airport, the restaurant later
and Annie (Miriam Gross has it too) – dark
hair, very white teeth, a charming regard, neat
features.

We proceed towards Apartment 8, past closed
doors and glass-enclosed gardens of house-
plants – as we would call them. Our apartment
is delightful and large. Arched windows, sitting

room, bedroom, extra bedroom, high window-less studio room, kitchen already with provisions – next morning I notice that everything is firmly labelled MEAT and DAIRY, according to the Kosher rules, and resolved hastily not to let down the side by mixing the two up.

We go to the Mishkenot restaurant, along the outside cloister which is even more monastic. This side has Hebrew numerals only. We memorise ours, which I describe as Sideways Dustbin, while H. neurotically tries to write it down. The restaurant is crowded and full of clearly jolly people. Both of us now exhausted, me rather sick. But the jolly manager (Moshe Pe'er, tho' I think him at first to be Mr. Pierre, which is how he introduces himself) finds us a quiet table. We eat hot hors d'oeuvres and veal and drink Israeli white wine – rather light and pleasant.

H. talks about his instruction for Bar Mitzvah, two nights a week learning Hebrew. "I haven't thought about it for years." How astounded his parents were by his gesture of revolt against the formal religion two years later. How they have mellowed. (Harold of course sent them on one or two trips to Israel when asked.)

We return to our Sideways Dustbin (H. points out the little Talmudic scroll outside, however) and can't get in, so round by many steps, knocking at locked gates – naturally, security is still with us.

In. I still read. Eban, having reached 1967, which only emphasises the peace and the newness of Mishkenot. H. reads the *Jerusalem Post* (which has a long profile of Golda Meir in it).

We are both absolutely exhausted.

Tuesday 9 May

Tuesday 9 May

Brilliant hard sunshine one senses from an early hour outside the silvery white blind over the arched window, and the traffic roars on the big road beneath Mishkenot. I peek up at the castle wall which I now realise is where the Jordanian guns perched before '67 threatening the poor (literally) Jews in the Mishkenot area. I visualise wretched black-clad figures scuttling about, reconciling themselves to the fact that every now and then an arbitrary gun will blow them out of this world. But scuttling in the same place every day all the same.

We make a breakfast of sweet bread and strawberry jam and coffee. The view from Mishkenot from where I now sit, in the outside cloister, stretches to the desert? or the sea? In the considerable heat, first up to the bank which contains, among numerous notices, two of interest:

1) WHAT YOU CAN DO FOR ISRAEL — AN IDEALISTIC NOTICE ABOUT CONTRIBUTIONS.

2) TOURISTS — MEETING AT 6 PM AT X HOTEL ABOUT POSSIBILITIES FOR INVESTMENT IN ISRAEL.

Hotel next door for Israeli beer (Americans in the preponderance, no sense of being in Israel). Then, armed only with a little paper map, we walk down hill and up dale to the Old City.

Entering the New Gate and finding ourselves immediately in another Arab world — for this is what it is, despite notices like LATIN PATRIARCHATE RD — is an extraordinary experience. The emptiness of the area outside the castle walls and the teeming scene within (like an operatic set with a colourful chorus strolling about) adds to the strangeness. We walk rather bemused, but straight down a narrow way marked DAVID. Shops on left and right and soon we are under arches and thus shaded in a sort of endless commercial catacomb, kaftans, eastern blouses, gold souvenirs of Islamic nature, even sheepskin waistcoats, with eager shopkeepers all cast out of the *Arabian Nights* (operatic version), also masses of vegetables, piles of peppers, red and green, tomatoes, bananas which look nice massed in the distance, rather frightening near to – I am suddenly terrified of being stranded here and forced to eat them! A nightmare of slight claustrophobia and hygiene. Then – "Look," says H., pointing up. A soldier with a large gun is sitting on the roof above the crowd. What is he on the lookout for? We haven't the faintest idea. "A familiar face in the crowd," suggests H. And soon we are at a police post being searched, before finding ourselves in an open space at the end of the Old City, with open and strange country beyond. Where are we? We furrow our brows desperately wondering whether this is the Jordan frontier?? Crazy, of course it isn't. But where was it?

The depth of our basic ignorance about obvious facts here hits us again and again during this strange morning. We were rather like moon-explorers in both history and politics, especially as H. won't have a guide (I think rightly – he would be maddened and so learn nothing) and relies on me to dig up knowledge from my thin memory. Actually it turns out later we were at the Wailing Wall. But H. definitely felt no atavistic twinge here – I am on the lookout for twinges. For that matter I am not going to feel any twinges, half an hour later, at the Via Dolorosa, beyond noting the name. But the latter is religion – maybe H. should at least have sensed *something* at the wall? Wistful notion. We really just see piles of police barricades. Up some guarded steps to a vast Mosque-dominated area. It seems rather deserted.

We sit in the shade beneath a stray arcade. A charming little silent Arab girl in a striped cotton school smock, smiling through a gap tooth, comes and sits behind us. She won't speak but seems friendly.

Kicking off our shoes, and H. having laboured back to get tickets (slight protest at both activities, shoes and tickets), we enter the central Mosque with its garish colours outside, its vast gleaming dome, via the soldiers lounging outside. While I await H.'s return, I read a notice about behaviour in the Mosque:

ATTENTION TO PROPER BEHAVIOUR ACCORDING TO THE LOCAL AUTHORITIES IS MANDATORY OBLIGATORY – ISRAEL POLICE.

In the Mosque it is indeed Keats' dim religious light, and jewel-like stained glass as in St. Agnes' Eve, but Islamic. And most beautiful. The garishness continues to the English eye in the bright red carpet inside, but you quickly forget that in the height and quiet. Also the emptiness. In the grotto we find one Arab worshipper bowing and murmuring. Hardly anyone else at all. In the centre, behind a wooden barricade we discover a low rocky plateau. This turns out to be a portmanteau rock of many religions and myths. "Where Abraham went to sacrifice Isaac," a guidish voice tells another couple. Do I discern a twinge in Harold?

As we walk away through the Mosque area, towards the Fortress of Antonia (my choice for obvious reasons), I realise that this cannot any longer be a great place of Arabic Pilgrimage. Hence perhaps the emptiness?

A few more schoolgirls skip about outside the Antonia, and much grass and weeds grow. It is very very hot as we poke out of a narrow gate into what turns out to be the Via Dolorosa. Back we wend, passing a hotel of Arabic nature (I have another twinge of fear that I will be imprisoned there) through more mounds of kaftans, Islamic ornaments and vegetables with certain more Catholic *objets* in the Via Dolorosa and there, at last, the front doors of monasteries and churches with names like "Hospice of the Flagellation" etc.

Out by the Damascus Gate. A taxi to the King David Hotel, snack in the Dairy Shop (fried fish sandwich and beer = £8) and a swim in the pool for me as the afternoon begins to shade and cool.

Of course what we have done, once I study our guidebook, acquired in the Via Dolorosa (which incidentally is written by a Franciscan and is anti-Greek Orthodox tho' tolerant of Jews and Arabs), is pass straight through to the Arab Quarter, leaving the Jewish Quarter to the right, Catholic to the left. We were like lemmings. So much for either of our twinges.

I fall into a heavy sleep and at 8 p.m. we meet David Samuel at the restaurant for a drink which turns into dinner. Then a tour of the City in his car late at night. He brings with him Ina, working in a bookshop in Jerusalem. David Samuel (described by George Weidenfeld as the best of Anglo-Jewry, sensitive, intelligent "and Harold, I believe, will especially like him") is all these things. As well as having a strange resemblance to the Indian Vidia Naipaul, genetically hard to explain. We find we share a North Oxford background.

Odd remarks:

D.S.: "No, I shan't be going to the parade tomorrow: I hate parades."

Ina: "No, I haven't seen the Museum. I never go to Holocaust things" (to which he replies: "No, but this is done with great taste: a memorial of a vanished culture").

On military service: how he has gone back with a lower rank each time! (Mainly organising matters of a scientific nature.)

How the younger generation begin to use Hebrew, reading English books less. However, the Weizmann Institute of Science (which was founded before the State of Israel) has a policy of giving lectures in English if there is one person present who doesn't understand Hebrew – which may lead to a sudden switch for the lecturer at the last moment (he himself is bi-lingual from his boyhood).

D.S.: "After all, these people are going out into the world and they won't be using Hebrew in the States."

Tells us of the problems of scientific language in Hebrew – the Bible is combed for assistance. The word for the apparition of God, for example, since "He doesn't appear so much these days", is employed for electricity. Our tour shows us Gethsemane from above – "Probably all you need to see of it" – light shining on the onion domes of the churches there. And the closeness of the desert. Really just waiting outside Jerusalem. "No wonder the prophets saw visions there" – D.S. "A terrifying place." It's an echo of Teddy Sieff's amusing remark about Galilee: "No wonder the primitives believed Christ walked on the water", due to the strange motion of the waves. Obviously the longer you live in the Holy Land, the easier you find it to believe that the Bible both did – and didn't – happen.

Wednesday 10 May

Very hot. Hotter at 11 a.m. for Remembrance of the Dead (and also at 8 p.m. last night). A moving article in the *Jerusalem Post* by a father who has lost his only son – "No one left to call me Abba ever again."

H. thinks we should not go near the Old City for two days, since he has discovered the soldiers are not normally there, but are against paraded "incidents" during these two days of Independence.

He is right. Although the risks of a car crash in England are greater, he is still right. It would be an ostentatious and foolish risk to run. (This story turns out to be quite untrue. A Jerusalem rumour about Tel Aviv.)

We don't run it. (Although the Old City

seems unperturbed by our decision and hangs about sunlit and unsinister. Nor are there any Arab incidents: mainly celebratory incidents formed by Jews hitting each other on the head with squeaky plastic hammers – a Tel Aviv fashion – so loudly that an open-air concert there with Leontyne Price the great singer is virtually abandoned!) Other risks are run. In heat which seems greater than yesterday we toil round the supermarket crammed because of the coming holiday. This is much more like the Golders Green of my youth, just after the War, push, push, shove, shove, but a Mediterranean version. I feel anti-social; H. feels anti-everything, particularly as we can't get a trolley and toil about with milk (in plastic bag), juice and whisky – in short the minimum requirements! – rather hopelessly like a couple of hot and disagreeable ants. At Mishkenot they told us the supermarket will deliver, but there seems small chance of that in this confusion...However, unruffled by girl at paydesk, I approach English-speaking Israeli (blue eyes, tough physique, clearly just back from the front) to charm him into obeisance. I *almost* do...until he sees the size of our bag...

To us the Stone of Sisyphus; to him a source of laughter, nay ridicule. "Is that all? I can't ask my drivers to deliver *that*. They would laugh at me."

Even H. now becomes affected by the pioneer spirit and simply grabs his burden again. "Oh quite, quite, it's not as heavy as all that." And off we go, shoulders squared, only for H. to slump two minutes later outside the pioneer orbit, once more bowed and exhausted by an intolerable burden, the frailest Rabbi from the Warsaw Ghetto, squared shoulders quite forgotten…He is only cheered by buying an anti-mosquito machine, such as we enjoyed in Haiti, in the chemist.

We're having an easy day, as I'm not feeling too hot and the day is. So we leg it up to the King David, on a now familiar trail, for H. to have a beer. The bar once again quite empty in this non-drinking city. Its silence and lack of populace meet at least some of H.'s requirements as a drinking-place.

Then we go by taxi to the Rockefeller (Archaeological) Museum, all in the bright stone of the Holy Land. Deserted: archaeological remains, like alcohol, not popular. Charming and civil attendants. We contemplate a folded-up skeleton, 12–20,000 years old, and as we stroll through the Ages, Bronze, Iron and that sort of thing, the concentration of history *here*, as though this part of the world was some area furiously coveted by quarrelling children, strikes me anew. But as with children, you can't understand quite why they should want a particular, seemingly innocuous book…

After all, if the Jews are *not* the Chosen People, Christ *not* the Son of God, what makes this place the undoubted microcosm it is? It seems simpler – logically – to accept that they are and that he is! The other explanation, which I suppose would be strategic, is so much less convincing and doesn't account for the moral ferocity of the quarrels.

Among the remains, Aphrodite at her bath, heavy firm limbs, glows. The jostle continues. Solomon's manger – yes, really, for the horses from his palace. A little worse for the wear. A

Harold, aged 47, photographed by Antonia at the American Colony Club.

Antonia, aged 45, photographed by Harold.

Harold and Antonia with Teddy Kollek, the charismatic Mayor of Jerusalem who welcomed them.

The Yorkshire-born playwright David Mercer, prolific author of plays and films in the sixties and seventies, at the American Colony Club.

Dafna Mercer, Israeli-born wife of David.

Visit to the Dead Sea: (clockwise, from upper-left) Antonia in the foreground in hat; Antonia afloat; the organiser of the trip, Lois Sieff (left) – wife of Teddy Sieff, President of Marks & Spencer – and her friend Eileen Marmont, enjoying a refreshing beer on the shore with Harold.

Harold's cousin Moshe Ben Haim, with his son Yoni. Harold had not seen Moshe for over 30 years since he emigrated illegally to Israel, having fought for his native Britain in the Second World War.

Hirsh Goodman of the *Jerusalem Post* and Harold.

Masada, the strong-hold where the Jews held out against the Romans c.73 AD.

The Cableway, which took tourists up and down from Masada.

The mountaintop fortress of Masada where, according to the historian Josephus, the Jews were besieged by the Romans after the Fall of the Temple in 70 AD. They committed mass suicide when they were finally defeated.

The certificate Antonia acquired and filled in for Harold to commemorate his exciting, if traumatic, expedition to Masada.

Mishkenot Sha'ananim, Old City, Jerusalem: the guest house where Antonia and Harold stayed.

Via Dolorosa – Old City, Jerusalem, 1978 – said to be the path Jesus took on the way to his crucifixion.

Zubin Mehta, who conduct-ed at a special concert in Jerusalem commemorating the 30th Anniversary of Israeli Independence in 1978.

Rostropovich at home after performing with the Jerusalem Symphony Orchestra at the 30th Anniversary concert.

Jackie Kennedy, who was on a visit to Israel, 1978.

Shimon Peres, in 1984 Prime Minister and in 2007 President of Israel.

Peter Halban and Antonia – dinner at the Rockefeller Museum, Jerusalem. Peter escorted Antonia and Harold up Masada.

Harold's parents, Frances and Jack Pinter, in London; they had already visited Israel, at their own request, before Harold and Antonia did.

delicately carved crystal of an Emperor's head; which is not.

Back to Mishkenot. I've finished Eban and start to check back in Moshe Dayan's *Story of My Life*. H. starts to read Eban on '73 and quickly gets absorbed. I start to read Dayan on his Open Bridges policy and get absorbed too. But H. and I agree that we can only take so much of "Israel" before turning to other things. H. reads Martin Amis' *Success* and Emma Tennant's new novel *The Bad Sister*, both rather brilliant and unpleasant works of the imagination and sickness.

I continue to ponder on the whole problem of the brilliant military man as posed by Dayan. All the diplomatic Triple First Ebans in the world would not have saved Israel after 1948 from extinction.

It was 1967 which freed Israel from certain pressures. Yet now once again Dayan's "arrogant" values are attacked and obviously rightly so – until of course they are needed again to survive the dreadful yo-yo of Israel's existence. As if the *world* had decided that really unique among states, Israel must be a *moral* state... something no other state is expected to be!

In the evening an extraordinary experience which doesn't necessarily belong to Israel but happens to us here. We go to the Jerusalem Theatre, a large concrete-block building, National Theatre style, for a celebratory concert. We are handsomely seated tho' the long hand of Jonathan Miller (of all people!) stretches forth to ruffle H.

Director of theatre – a very tall man indeed in a safari suit: "I am so *delighted* to see you here. I never thought you would come. You see, Jonathan Miller explained you were frightened to come to Jerusalem."

H.: ???

Director: "For the effect it would have on your work…"

H.: !!!

Enough of that. The concert marked totally by the divine Rostropovich. He comes onto the stage, an unexpectedly tall and shambling figure, almost clown-like, his balding head and heavy rounded jaw which gives a faintly spastic air (a sort of Stanley from *The Birthday Party*) then he sits down, and you hardly think he's ready, the orchestra plays, he twists and turns, you want to tell him, warn him, "Rostropovich, they're *starting*!"

Then suddenly the most tremendous attack, a huge deep sawing noise from the forest. After which from then on, the concert is his… He plays as an encore Bach's Sarabande in G, which in an E.F. Benson-like way we heard him practising through our bedroom wall in the morning. It ends on a long note. He drew his bow across and held it, head bowed. In contrast to the end of the Haydn when he had jumped up, all Russian ebullience.

I was profoundly moved. I was with the silence. Afterwards, rather idiotically post-party 1 a.m., Harold and I argue about this one moment. It doesn't affect the experience. The party is given by an impresario called Victor Hochhauser and wife in a newly constructed studio-house close to Mishkenot. Mrs. Hochhauser is warm and gay, and drink including champagne actually flows (no drink at all at the theatre!). Israeli High Society, if that's what it is – later I hear Zubin Mehta, the great conductor, criticising this loudly in the Mishkenot restaurant – is rather fun. H. sits down with Teddy Sieff who asks if he may call him Harold, and tells him he has given so much money to Israel that he has hardly any left. Yet it is his whole life…Lights shine on the ash-tree outside and the twinkling lights towards the desert, the ever-present light-ed walls. A woman describing herself as the Mme. Furtseveya of Israel, i.e. Arts Minister: "I know your name. Tell me why?"

Me, pausing and stumbling: "Well, I'm a writer, sort of biographer."

She is not very satisfied.

H., *sotto voce*: "You should have said, 'Well, I left my husband for Harold Pinter and there was all this scandal in the newspapers'…"

Thursday 11 May

My bumps and patches are worse (the allergy).

We get up early-ish and trek up to the King David and go to Jericho and the Dead Sea with Lois Sieff. The journey is quite extraordinary. One moment the environs of Jerusalem, newly built if small houses, then with one stride comes the desert. As though an invisible weed-killer had been poured on all habitations beyond a certain point. And immediately Bedouins appear, black clad, moving slowly and wearily with black goats. We also see a few (black) tents crouching on the dusty hills. The road, built since 1967, is fast and implacable, and we stop only at various military checkpoints – or rather slow down to be waved on.

Our driver (a handsome Israeli whom H. describes as innocent – not a term of praise, as
will appear): "The Arabs have yellow licences
and they don't stop us because we have white
ones." H. and I both imagine that Arabs *here*
are forced to have different licences, a rather
horrifying yellow star system. But of course
he's referring to the Arabs from Jordan which
is after all quite reasonable. Nevertheless his
"us and them" attitude to Jews and all Arabs is
quite marked. It goes with the absolutely evi-
dent fact that this is an area inhabited by Arabs
and occupied by Jews. The security reasons
may be perfect. It is nevertheless a fact.

We see two Israeli "settlements", one with
so much barbed wire and lookouts it is like a
prison. Lois Sieff: "They are really military
posts, not settlements. But of course Begin's aim
would be to make them settlements."

Can it be right? Jericho, whatever it was, is
now a totally Arab town. I think of American
settlers in the West and the native Indians. What
is the right anyway?

Apart from that, the desert is fierce, hot and
predatory, the verdant oasis of Jericho all the

more remarkable. Suddenly here is an African town as I have known them, bougainvillea, flame-trees, avenues.

A Jericho dig (they look in vain for the walls…) is rather boring. Besides our innocent guide, who will keep telling us Bible stories with an air of imparting totally new information, is driving H. quite mad. In vain he tries to stop him telling us about Lazarus ("This man died and Jesus Christ, who was a Jew…").

Lois lightens the atmosphere by being very jolly about H.'s sensitivities.

We arrive at the Dead Sea where a Dead Sea beer in the strange cafe/bar makes a new man of H. It also revives a millionaire's pleasant wife called Eileen Marmont, along for the ride, last met by me in Barbados.

The Dead Sea, blue and inviting from a distance beneath its hills is, close to, a mess of mud and salt pans. The atmosphere is odd. You can't go further than this ornate-looking cafe and changing rooms. There are only road-blocks visible otherwise: "ISRAELI DEFENCE. NO ADMITTANCE". Tho' more hotels, says Lois, at the end of the lake where Germans love to go for the mud. The mud is formidable and is indeed my main impression of the swim. I'm determined to do it but otherwise the make-shift squalor of the changing rooms and freshwater showers combined with heat is fairly nasty.

Lois gallantly walks to the water with me (we chat about our mutual friend Ushy Adam) and I gingerly immerse myself, still in my straw hat. Yes, I do float. Yes, I have swum in the Dead Sea. Decision later to send for doctor for allergies and much telephoning by H.

Off to the evening outdoor concert, bearing our blanket. At one point Teddy Kollek, the Mayor of Jerusalem, spies us and says: "You have platform seats" but when we don't take them is undismayed. We wend our way through thousands of people – literally, 10,000 – and as if by magic find Michael Kustow from the National Theatre. We all sit on a rock together in the rift valley below the castle walls, with built-up domed stage. It's an extraordinary feeling. The night air cools. The people listen with rapt attention so that any disturbance like one motor-bike seems extraordinary. Rostropovich plays, Jean-Pierre Rampal (flautist, ducking and bowing with his pipe like a huge Pan), Leontyne Price sings, Zubin Mehta conducts. This I feel is a peculiarly Israeli experience, this dedication to music, which has brought forth this tribute from these great artists.

In Tchaikovsky's 1812 symphony real cannons roar beneath us, the only firing – tho' soldiers are everywhere and several people murmur, "an opportunity for Arafat". Indeed the thought has crossed my mind that, wedged in a natural stadium, we would be excellent massed targets either as victims or hostages.

But all is peace. A reception at Mishkenot, outdoors. First we take a drink from Lia Van Leer, Film Archivist. The stars come in. I watch Leontyne Price watching Barbra Streisand on television in a Zubin Mehta show from Los Angeles. She admires the talent, the huge voice; one can also see her visibly scorning the art. She teases Mehta: "You're deserting us." Her face is massive, the great false eyelashes on the same scale. She is most *soignée*.

At the reception the soldiers, very very young, at last relax and drink at the (small) bar. Bed by 1.30, after H. and I have had a long talk about plans. His need for spontaneous plans and so forth. Whatever they are! I feel a spontaneous need for bed...

Friday 12 May

In hot weather – and poor H. feeling a malaise from it – the chores of life such as going to the bank and chemist for medicines prescribed by v. nice Israeli doctor Evan Pas (formerly Gluckstein) seem arduous. Doctor incidentally prescribes exactly the same medicines as my London specialist Harvey Baker…always comforting! He spent 10 years on a kibbutz in Galilee and knows Harold's cousin "Moshe Ben Haim" – an interesting, handsome figure who now keeps popping up, last seen by H. about 30 years ago. Now, who knows? Perhaps after life on the kibbutz he is still a very handsome figure, tanned and slim…

H. collapses in the King David bar which is cool and I go off to the Old City about noon to see the Church of the Holy Sepulchre: a little Catholicism I feel will not come amiss. In the noon heat even the Arabs selling kaftans, their sisters, gold souvenirs etc. etc. are somewhat torpid and their cries: "Look, Mrs., I want to tell you something" lack energy. Several shops are closed. I find the Church of the Holy Sepulchre easily, pattering through agreeable squares with Byzantine arches and pillars. The church itself lies in a similar courtyard with fine Byzantine doors. There is a quietness and a tranquillity, here too, almost a silence (only one guide, not importunate and showing me his "anthorisation"). I am incidentally transported to a very different country, Ethiopia, visited 14 years ago, in the dusty interior, the odd carpet, the odd oil painting dark and holy on the walls, a bearded priest in long black robe sitting impassively. A few Arab-looking boys stroll about – Christian Arabs, I realise. They prove to be quiet and charming and to my surprise do not accost me.

I wander round the outside of the basilica. One priest does try to show me a glimpse of "the rock". But the various chapels, all quite deserted, all belong to different sects according to the guidebook: Latin, Greek, Russian, Syrian, Coptic, Jacobite and Ethiopian Christians. The rules laid down for ownership and guardianship are most elaborate.

The first impression is therefore of the immense separateness of Christianity, the concentration on these barriers. Even the guidebook, written by a Franciscan, is virulent against the Greeks.

But there is also, rather to my surprise, a feeling of mystery here. Something. Not to do with the facts of Calvary and the tomb – if this is the place (the Anglicans of course go for somewhere quite different found by General Gordon!) – but to do with worship over centuries. And the ultimate unknowability of all things to do with it – strange sad guess-work.

I stumble down steps and find a crypt dedicated to the Holy Cross and St. Helena who found it, an obstinate engaging woman for whom I've always felt warmly. It's empty except for a renovating workman. Indeed a great deal of works are going on here, the subject, the guidebook assures me, of international argument and arbitration over years which must make them even slower than ordinary works. There is another spare crypt below with a statue of St. Helena. I finish off up the "steps of Calvary" to what is either a Greek or Orthodox chapel (it turns out to be both) and light a candle bought from a majestic priest in charge. His eyes are flashing but unseeing. Later I see his photograph in the paper – Father Daniel, guardian of the Greek Orthodox shrine.

In the afternoon Lia Van Leer takes me to Bethlehem. She's a very pleasant woman, Bessarabian/Rumanian married to a Dutch Jew called Vim, an amazing adventurous figure who seems to have done everything everywhere, mainly in his own aeroplane.

I had intended *not* to go to Bethlehem but I'm glad I do. The hilly country is an illustration of the Bible which I hadn't appreciated. The tourists simply aren't there, perhaps because it is late afternoon altho' there is plenty of room for their coaches in "Manger Square". The tourist centre is hideous too. But the church again spare and rather mysterious. Once again the world of Eastern Christianity. One priest in tall black hat who sells us a candle for my intention, with total lack of interest. One polite guide, easily rebuffed. Some items round the walls, some of which Lia says are precious, some evidently not. Endless hanging lamps (a feature too of the Holy Sepulchre).

In the Grotto, the Cave of the Birth. Some people kneeling and some candles, more of the latter than the former. We are joined by a party of Arab Christian boys and a priest who recites what I think is the Hail Mary in Arabic. In the shop too, the Arab Christian old man is gentle and charming.

In the evening, dinner at Lia and Vim's house which goes on till 1.30. Hanna Maron – Israel's Peggy Ashcroft – a most sympathetic woman who has played in *Landscape* reads from her Hebrew copy in a low and lovely voice. Plus pauses.

Vim: "Why don't you read a soliloquy or something, Hanna?"

Hanna: "This is a soliloquy. These are pauses."

Vim: "Oh, I thought it was the other fellow."

H. raises the subject of Israeli-Arab education – the general consensus being that it is the Arab culture which prevents assimilation and this the Arabs are (naturally) granted. But it does prevent any proper integration at the earliest educational level, as for example we have at schools in England. Because with a different language, a different culture, Arabs given their own schools, how else can they grow up but as different peoples?

Incidentally the next night the director of a successful Israeli-Arab community centre in Haifa tells us most amusingly of his decision to appoint an Arab director. The perfect man was found, an Arab Christian with a family in Nazareth etc. etc. The only problem: the incredible, covetable sexuality of this man! Which makes for the most immense disruption in everybody's lives including that of his wife, his Dutch mistress, the Centre, and an 18-year-old

Muslim Arab girl whose two sisters (teacher and education officer respectively) vow to kill her in old-fashioned Muslim style. All parties take off to Colorado where our friend has wrangled this man a scholarship to get him out of Haifa and the chaos, ensuring, however, the girl wins out. But of course by now the Arab girl has a) married b) left her husband c) herself teaches at the University...

All this is by the way. On the Friday, talk is more sober. We are joined by David Harman who was an Intelligence Officer on the Golan Heights in both '67 and '73 and incidentally no relation to the Harmans who were my mother's family. An example of the Jews who used to exasperate my Unitarian grandfather, Nathaniel Harman, by taking his name on naturalisation. He thought it was unfair that they should start as Harman... Actually these Harmans were Russian, started as Garman, Harmon in England, Harman in Israel. David tells us of the complete chaos in '73 – traffic blocks of tanks one way and the wounded the other. One man, a sergeant, directing it and making a complete mess. He taps him on the shoulder to pull rank...it's the Dean of his

University. But the general impression of this evening is firstly immensely interesting. These are all highly intelligent people talking about vital things. As H. said: "Even with our cleverest friends, like Simon Gray and Tom Stoppard, we would have been talking about Bernard Levin and his beastly theatre reviews half the evening."

But then one sees the cleft stick in which they are caught. Liberals who must give the Arabs their own culture.

Me to David Harman, *sotto voce*: "Any other people would have first imposed military schooling on the occupied Israeli Arabs. Problem ends in a generation."

Fighters who must survive.

Saturday 13 May

Sabbath. You don't see much sign of it except in the Old City in the Jewish Quarter. Give or take the heat (better today) it's like Inverness on Sunday. Closed, shuttered and v. quiet. Otherwise it's a London Sunday, with tourists splashing in the King David pool.

We take a dip or rather I do, after our late night, and then on to the brunch at the American Colony Hotel. Lia showed me this yesterday and I know H. would enjoy its green-house appeal. We lunch from an enormous buffet, two whole curved fishes, decorated with monstrous eyes of olives and tomatoes looking at us in a reproachful way, as well as many other hors d'oeuvres, Turkish in feel like the rugs on the walls. We drink a bottle and a half of Mount Carmel white wine which we agree is just like water and discuss Emma Tennant's book. We agree that it *is* brilliant. Besides, after we've discussed it over a whole lunch, its compulsion can't be denied.

Lia arrives, like a good fairy, with her calm broad Rumanian face, and takes us off to the apartment of a young Israeli girl named Michie Ronnen who lives with Lia's architect. We believed her to be married to him but as she refers to him as "my partner for life" we realise, rather paradoxically, that he is not necessarily this…Or rather she had a partner for life before.

Michie is beautiful in the new Israeli style, white teeth, wonderful brown straight hair, olive skin, light eyes. Nothing of the old-style Jewish beauty about her. Flat and pretty figure, for example, no bosom.

We learn that she was on the cover of *Time* for the Israeli 25th Anniversary, being then 25 years old, in a uniform with a gun, smiling.

She is now, says Lia, sadder. Perhaps that's her private life. She is a charming compassionate creature talking about her psychiatric work among the soldiers on the Golan Heights. Many of them who try to get out of the army on mental grounds because it's three years' hard slog do not realise that they will probably not get into universities or get jobs afterwards – mental breakdowns *not* respectable here.

Back to Mishkenot where I'm now reading *O Jerusalem!* and am in the midst of the siege of Jerusalem, the horrifying ordeals of the Haganah trying to relieve the Jewish settlements by convoy and being stoned and blown to pieces by the Arab ambushers, unbelievably callous behaviour.

H. reads David Plante's book, *The Family*.

Another interesting gathering at Lia's, the aforesaid director, his artist wife, v. attractive modelled happy face with short thick black hair (older and thus not the new Israeli beauty). We discuss Begin.

Rather pathetically they all say: "But don't the English understand he's not *elected*?" Details, almost indignant, follow. Eight percent of votes, compromise, etc. etc. The failure of the long-reigning party.

The truth is that even H., who is, in England, rather obsessed with Begin and reads out his speeches from time to time in tones of angry horror (I think they confirmed his secret nightmares about Israel) didn't realise this! So how are the English people as a whole to take it in? And anyway, in a gloomy way, it's not the point. The point is he is their Prime Minister and he is doing great harm to the Israeli image at the same time as a new generation arises to whom the Palestinian refugees, not the victims of the Holocaust, are the underdogs. It's a bad combination.

We walk back through the cool night, past the statue of the soldier outside one of the artistic houses. It's like Greece, a wind, some stars, a moisture in the air.

H. says he is very happy to be in Israel. Earlier

he has said that the real reason he did not come here all these years is not in fact covered by his curt remark to Vim: "Well, I'm here now." He feared to dislike the place, the people.

Now he doesn't; he is very happy at both the place and above all the intelligence we find.

H.: "What I mean is, I see no reason why we shouldn't come here again. Here to Israel."

Sunday 14 May

H. to Vim Van Leer: "Do you always carry a gun?" (We have been rather startled to observe a small but unmistakeable black gun at his hip.)

Vim: "Always when I'm in Arab Country. I wouldn't like to lose my guests. For example it would be sad to return and say, 'Pity about old Antonia!'"

Privately I note that it would be the non-Jewish member of the party that perished...

We are at the Herodion, near Bethlehem, but very different country. This is (at last) the land of the Bible rather than Israel. Gone are the modern stone villas of suburban Bethlehem. Arabs "abide" with their sparse flocks – as Vim constantly reminds us of the Old Testament phrase, satirically — and although near the mountain there are bright clear green fields of an olive shade, on the other side I can only think of Shelley's "Ozymandias" — "the lone and level sands stretch far away". Except of course they are not sands but sandy mountains, endless and in seeming perfect formations.

How to describe this, I think? Just as I am resolving that H.'s infinitely greater talents will have to be employed, his voice breaks into my thoughts: "How will you write about this in your Diary?" I tell him that I am hoping that *he* will be the painter...For it is a question of colour and I daresay if I was a painter I would see what exactly the colour relationships are which make it so beautiful. Something I suspect of this bright green and darker olive, shading out but still with green somewhere to the mountains' sandy ranges, and there is pink here too, subtly preventing anything from being brown or drab. Extraordinary. Quite missing the blue and purple at the heart of all Scottish mountain scenes.

When you do see the bright turquoise blue the Arabs use on shutters and doors (to keep out the Evil Eye) it gives you the shock which the Evil Eye is presumably supposed to receive. You blink.

The Herodian is in Vim's opinion a blunt fortress, unrefined. I am much impressed on the contrary by its position, carved into the top of the mountain, an excavated castle, its living quarters recalling the great mediaeval Norman strongholds of Pevensey etc., its pillars the might of Rome. H. is also impressed by it. Incidentally I have been secretly marvelling at his ability to stand the height, which I put down to his Israeli "geniality".

Moshe Pearlman (writer to generals and others) comes for a drink. Last seen skiing in 1973 with George Weidenfeld, Lallie Weymouth, her children, Jonathan and Nicky Berry, an oddly assorted party. He is the same cheerful chatty chap.

H.: "Would you carry a gun in Arab Country?"

Moshe: "No, certainly not." Pause. "I might be shot at, mind you, but I wouldn't expect to be."

More talk of Begin whom Moshe at least makes sound human (having known him in government).

We take Van Leers to supper at Fink's, a tiny Jewish restaurant owned by a Mr. Rothschild (no relation), once the centre of the British Press Corps and Intelligence. Still intimate and agreeable. Van Leer and Mr. Rothschild have the lugubrious conversation of old men who have known each other a long time, each being rather surprised to find the other so healthy.

Van Leer, however, *is* incredibly healthy and tells us of his first marriage to Gerda, who leaves him for a Swiss cowhand called Ernst who knows all the cows by their names, "Rosie, Schmosie, and Posie and so on…" We speculate that this turn-down has transformed Van Leer to the buccaneer crop-sprayer he is…

Anyway we really like the bold Van Leers very much and they have been our entry into the enjoyment of Israeli life, to tell the truth.

Monday 15 May

The dreaded (by H.) 6.30 rise to go to Masada. We are on parade by 7.30 for Peter Halban, son of Aline Berlin, step-son of Isaiah, to take us, and there is a faint wind blowing. He assures us we are lucky. In Masada terms, where temperatures can rise to 100 even at this time of the year, it will be a cool day.

The ride down the Jericho road is, as before, fascinating, so quickly comes the desert and one man heading towards it with a camel – although as Peter points out, the English word "wilderness" is really better suited for this flint and scrub. South down the banks of the Dead Sea for miles in his fast smooth Alfetta. He turns out to be a most agreeable companion, three years in Israel, a member of the Peace Now movement, but also points to the land round us (at Jericho) and says: "This would be Palestine. Is it truly a viable state?"

Me: "Only with millions of Arab money…"

Peter: "Precisely."

But it's the geography of it which hits one, as geography always does, on the spot, *not* in maps (hence boredom of theoretical subject!), so close to the busy burgeoning Jerusalem: how can anyone expect the Israelis to welcome a *state* set up by Arafat and his murderous boys here?

Then we swoop away into a more timeless scenery. To our right rise up sharply the high reddish cliffs which to my excitement turn out to have contained the Dead Sea Scrolls. You can even see the round caves where the shepherds found them, the actual caves. It is easy to im-agine, because of its dry timelessness, that the scrolls just dried and dried and dried. And re-mained and remained and remained.

H. gets v. excited when he sees a deer watching us with pricked-up ears from a rock (apparent-ly the desert deer are rare). I am less impressed, only because in Scotland you get used to deer watching you from rocks – but as H. would say, we are not in Scotland now. He reflects, he tells me later: "That deer has seen a thing or two!" Or a deer just like it. The Dead Sea is now a vivid cerulean blue, turning even to aquamarine later in the day. The mountains of Moab on the opposite bank are visible in this – allegedly – cool atmosphere. (I suppose it's about 80? We have the air conditioning on.) It is difficult to believe Peter's tales of flash floods in the winter, tho' the roads have clearly been washed away by the wadis regularly. We pass a kibbutz and later see its works, spread-out fields of tomatoes and so forth, done by trickle irrigation. The guest house of the kibbutz, very smart, looks vaguely Swiss with its mountain background, plus some flame-trees.

Then our first glimpse of Masada. This first sight of the rock fortress, shaped like an enormous anvil standing out from the mountain range (but in fact level with it), is the most amazing thing we see. Against some stiff competition. But it is: in one gasp one is recalled to the heroes of Masada, their deaths, the idea of the last redoubt – any last redoubts. I am recalled in my mind to Machu Picchu, last redoubt of the Incas, a green and savage version.

However, the actual journey up to Masada, by cable-car, is more characterised by the pettier side of tourism than magnificence of thought or deed. We have got here early to avoid the tourists as well as the heat. Nevertheless vast coaches are already drawn-up. Several bear the label: "United Zionist Federation of South Africa" which, to be honest, does seem to contain within it a lot of rather menacing concepts!

Nor are the cable-car's contents better than you would expect, rather worse, in tiny hats, too tiny for their big heads, with ISRAEL on them and a funny face, and plump women in v. short sun-dresses. And the loud voices which make Harold flinch.

H. puts his head down and endures. Also of course the height. Peter has warned us that the last 30 metres after the car will be a little vertiginous, but Harold is fairly confident after his yesterday's triumph that he will manage. Actually it *is* vertiginous and he does find it so, but by sticking to the inner rail and being sandwiched by Peter and me, does manage it.

So here we are. It's enormous, the great top, a place where people could easily have lived for several years, one instantaneously understands that (I think of the great mediaeval British strongholds, also whole towns inside, like Pembroke Castle). Later I discover that Herod even had it covered with fertile soil in the days of its glory. Beneath and far away spreads out the Dead Sea, and the remains of the Roman encampments which were built to siege it. But we are now companions of the mountains and on an eye-level with them. An exhilarating feeling.

Otherwise it is of course not so much the traces of Herod's splendid palaces and mosaic-ed bathrooms which move one (although the lack of figures in Herod's mosaics *is* interesting – "not otherwise a very religious man," says Peter dryly) – as the traces of the later simpler occupants. We don't get into the plain little synagogue because it is full of praying and watching tourists. At first Peter, who has turned out to be almost as intolerant as H. of such creatures, derides them for their hypocrisy, and stamps away.

Later he decides they are sincere because they have some vestments with them. However, one way or another we don't go in.

I am thus left to be moved by the simple Byzantine chapel, still standing, of the fifth-century monks who came here last of all. And all the time, my imagination inflamed by a short version of the Masada story in the guidebook, I worry over the characters of the two women who decided to survive the general suicide. Survivors? Yes, but what sort of survivors – determined eccentrics against the general will, intelligent or primitive? I am much attracted to the notion of these women. When down from Masada, I think wistfully that before I met Harold, I would have ambitiously tried to write a play about them, to learn that way.

The sight of the Roman rampart which creeps up behind the rock like an animal's back with a vertebrae, a sluggish pterodactyl perhaps, is equally stirring of the imagination. How ghastly to watch that *thing* inexorably creeping towards you, over two years, unable to stop it for all the stones hurled down in China. Or rather Masada.

All this time poor H. has distinctly not been feeling well, the last vertiginous rise having evidently shaken him more than I realised. Also the heat – on this "cool" day! – is already terrific (it's about 10.30 a.m.). He sits down in one of the shaded areas for tourists, despite the presence of the braying guides around us, which with their hateful microphones, is definitely not helping.

Now for the descent. It's definitely much much worse from the beginning because we are supposed to trek down on the *outside*. With no inside rail. H. takes a look, hesitates. I, who do not realise that at this point he has glimpsed the abyss itself, simply see him stagger slightly, turn white and half fall, half sit down on the step. It is a terrible moment. I *have* to believe that he will get down, we *will* get down, because if I don't, he won't and no one will. This is no time for trembles and fears on my part. H. goes back inside into the cool and dark shed and murmurs: "I think I could go down the inside" ie the upward track – which of course is filled by upward-coming tourists.

Peter Halban is wonderful. Totally calm. We don't discuss the possibility of what happens if H. *can't* come down...I mean, does he live up here? Like the Zealots? Till the Romans come again. H. then brilliantly takes *off* his spectacles, and at the same moment I grasp his hand in an enormously firm grip and, trying to exude strength from my hand to his hand, *lead* him down the inward track. Peter goes ahead, waving aside indignant tourists in many languages, a task I think he enjoys.

We get down to the cable-car. In the car H., sweating heavily and looking extremely ill, still no spectacles, staggers onto the solitary bench. It is occupied by another, heavy-set, man who begins: "As an Irish-American, may I salute a fellow Britisher?" It would only happen to H.... In the end Peter and I turn round and forcibly shut him up. "Why, is he ill or something?" queries the man in a baffled and rather hurt but still very grating voice.

So we are down.

H. later: "You know I told you I didn't know what the next stage of vertigo was. Well now I know. Coldness. Nausea."

Me: "You were a hero – you got down!"

H.: "With your hand."

He gives me a copy of Yadin's splendid *Masada* inscribed "To Antonia, the girl who got me down alive".

I spend much of the rest of the day reading and thinking about Masada, having at last finished *O Jerusalem*. (It had compelled to the end, particularly the story of Notre Dame Convent, full of enclosed nuns, *Soeurs reparatrices*, who had not even *seen* a man for 50 years. Occupied four times by Jews and Arabs in 48 hours, then off to the Latin Patriarchate for the immediate continuance of their prayers in the hall there, turning their chairs to the wall and immediately singing a holy French hymn to Our Lady – 15 May, today's date – "Oh May is the loveliest month, the month of Our Lady's birth".)

Josephus reveals that one of the surviving women of Masada was a relation of Eleazer, the leader, and indeed "intelligent beyond the run of women". But Eleazer's speech about the freedom of a chosen death and the unlimited weapon of immortality in their cause (by which he persuaded his people to commit suicide) is

73

such as to convince me he is right. It is a speech about the triumph of the spirit. Did these women then reject spiritual survival for sheer survival? Did they have more imagination, or actually rather less?

We discuss the topic with David Mercer who, with his young Israeli wife Dafna (a new Israeli beauty, white teeth, delicate figure), gives us dinner. As I seized on the women, David seizes on Eleazer's speech.

David: "With my ex-Communist background, I have a horror of people impelled to do things en masse by the power of rhetoric."

H., I think, is sympathetic to the Zealots, who preferred death at their own hands to slavery and subjugation, and death at the hands of the Romans. We eat at a restaurant in Ein Karim, former Arab Quarter now middle-class professional Jewish, termed by its owners, doubtless accurately, as "the only true Hungarian restaurant in the Middle East". Then two friends of the Mercers, an Argentinian-Chilean Jewish Professor of English and warm ample wife, collect us. They are living in one of these done-up Arab houses. The air of the ascent is starry and we feel curiously faraway. It is the quarter of the Visitation (I note that even the Professor can't resist telling me of the oft-told tale as if I'd never heard of it). We discuss bringing up children in the Jewish *tradition* without Jewish religion, as David hopes to bring up Becky Mercer, his daughter by Dafna, thus half Jewish.

David: "But I also hope to give her good Yorkshire working-class Trade Unions traditions too."

Me: "How old is she?"

David: "Three."

Me, solemnly: "It is more than time for that, David."

Nevertheless I agree with him profoundly on both counts, Jewish and non-Jewish, whatever my equivalents of the Yorkshire T.U. movement would be.

Bed by 1.30. We discuss David. A serious and above all an intelligent man, as H. says. Has found a sort of happy Purgatory in Haifa with Dafna, for some of the year, and it seems to work.

Tuesday 16 May

V. hot day – the Khamsin wind said to be persecuting us from the desert.

Lunch at the American Colony Club with the Mercers and Peter Halban. Conversation does get around to Bernard Levin this time – the effect of David and Harold together? But David does talk also interestingly about Bettelheim's book on the kibbutz principle and how the peer group was deliberately substituted for the claustrophobic hold of the Jewish family. Peter contradicts this fiercely: the communal care of children was economic in the early days. In any case parents on his kibbutz saw more of their children certainly than upper-class English parents and hard-working, working-class mothers.

David: "Yes, but whatever the practice, that was the theory..."

And I remain worried by the physical divorce of babies as early as six months.

The food is also disgusting in my view, brown fried fish or grilled. The geraniums and ambiance still delightful.

I get myself to the Shrine of the Book, a wing of the Israel Museum, feeling dehydrated and have to imbibe cold tea in hot and empty cafeteria. Israeli kindness. Apparently sullen attendant goes for miles to fetch me a fresh lemon, "You want lemon?"

I had not even thought of it. There is a determination here that things should be right.

The Shrine of the Book, a specially built building like a white mushroom outside, an Egyptian (sorry) tomb inside, repays the visit, especially so soon after Masada. Here are the scrolls – or rather fragments – from those days' high-up caves. And also "artefacts". As always it's the ordinary which is the most impressive to the simple mind. "Just like ours."

So I gaze portently at a straw basket *exactly* like the one which carries my picture-hanging equipment at home, and is 2000 years old.

Best buy: paperback of Edmund Wilson's book of the Dead Sea Scrolls. On the way back to Mishkenot a good if depressing view of Jerusalem – the modern skyscraper city spread out before one, white rather than beautiful.

But E. Wilson transports me. I remember my fierce interest in the subject years ago, now re-aroused. His measured take-you-by-the-mind prose is also refreshing and magisterial after Lapierre/Collins' journalese and Yadin's simplicity. I am swept away into another world of discovery and controversy, existing at exactly the same time as the bloody fights of *O Jerusalem!* (incidentally H. is by now quite hooked on this book in my place).

Supper at the Rockefeller Museum "hosted" by the Baron Edmond de Rothschild although there is in fact no sign of him. Jackie Kennedy *is* here – which is an odd feeling – but I don't get to meet her and in a way don't particularly want to and mix things. That dramatic life when I did know her seems a world away from this one. It's our first rather dull evening but I had expected many more like this. Even so, the incredibly balmy night, the supper under the stars in the piazza by the water, thick lavender growing, a stone lion, small goldfish, the bill carvings, Solomonic lumps and pillars, all make it quite tolerable. The company, if examined, is rich-American-museum-patron type. But Teddy Kollek wanders about in his open-shirt and later awards birthday cakes rather impatiently to various 80-year-old donors.

"Will you stand up to get your cakes." The old men, small and smiling, obediently bob up and down. As H. points out, there is also a pleasing austerity in the one bottle of wine, one dish cold buffet and simple fruit. None of the waste and gaudiness of banquets for English charities. Teddy Kollek wants it all for Jerusalem.

Later, over Israeli champagne ("The President's sparkling wine"), cold and light, H. says re our visit: "I definitely *am* Jewish. I know that now. But of course that makes it more complicated. I am also English. And this is an Arab town."

Me: "I could live here in every way except one, and that's not being Jewish." This is a *Jewish* State. That's its strength and foundation. I would never be part of it in the most real way.

It's an academic discussion of course but an interesting one.

Wednesday 17 May

Quite a day! For one thing, *intensely* hot and we learn later that we have passed through Jericho at 43 degrees, to say nothing of the Jordanian desert on the West Bank, when even the life-giving wind in the car was like blowing flames. But that's not the point, although when we first meet Hirsh Goodman, the young military correspondent of the *Jerusalem Post*, at Lia's for breakfast, it seems as if it's going to be. He talks merrily of Tiberias, Galilee, Safat, the Golan Heights, all places we have rejected as being too far away and taking too much time after days of anxious cogitation. "The slow day burns" in H.'s phrase in his first poem to me in Paris, and I long suddenly *not* to be in the powers of this energetic young man in an un-air conditioned car, touring settlements full of aggressive and hot people. My spirits are low but I feel I cannot suddenly be the one who says "Fains go…"

As it happens we have the most interesting day so far, an incredibly rich day, not the least of it being the personality of Hirsh Goodman. He's South African – Jewish, naturally – and not only the combination reminds one of Ronnie Harwood but also his charm and enquiring energy. He has abnormally long and thick eyelashes above very dark brown eyes alive with liberal questionings and doubts – and also jokes. Six years on a kibbutz, now married to a fellow former South African who teaches, he has two young children.

Hirsh: "I ask myself whether I have the right to bring up two children in this state, in a constant state of war?"

And he suddenly speaks of Madeira, "so beautifully dull", and what it would be like *not* to live in Israel where you imbibe argument and even decisions of conscience every day just as you clean your teeth. (This we have observed.)

Equally he regrets the drying-up of idealistic

immigration here from the U.S. and the U.K.: "The Jews who come here now tend to be the ones with nowhere to go." He himself is clearly an extremely idealistic person – one can see what tortured problems the idea of a state founded in any way on the subjugation of the Arabs would pose.

Meanwhile the red-hot wilderness whizzes by (he drives very fast, tho' very skilfully). And we do see for ourselves for the first time exactly what the extraordinary achievement of the mad, and I mean mad, Israelis has been. For it must be madness to come as they have come to a country without water, shade or even *soil* and there is this arid desert contained, don't forget, by hostile Arab mountains (from which shells emerge in the air, terrorists by night) and yet insist on growing the green vegetables and flowers of Hertfordshire and Worcestershire. And here we do see the patches of green field, even flowers under sun-shades, as though plonked down suddenly by an irrational finger. Nothing to do with the surrounding terrain at all. But of course they have hardly been planted down. Hardly. The kibbutzim houses are on a ridge to the left, and we pass the odd tractor. To the right a double row of barbed wire above the narrow Jordan creek – it is no more than that – and gravel raked nightly to test it for terrorist footprints. To the far right the mountains of Jordan remain serene and apparently indifferent.

And all the time the burning heat rises and blows and puffs. I begin to wonder with interest if I shall survive, spraying my face rather feebly with Evian water and looking at the patches of incomprehensibly irrigated land. When we get to the old pre-1967 Israel of course the land is greener, big trees rise up like cypresses, and vine crops, yes, vines. But the greenest feel and sight of all is the lake of Galilee itself, glimpsed blue and hazy at Tiberias which seems an exquisite town to us from the desert. Indeed I am suddenly seized with the most romantic thoughts of Christ's mission, and how happy he must have been in this comparatively fertile paradise, walking on this nice refreshing lake, having his picnics on the mount and so forth. How he must have hated going to that hot Jerusalem! Well, of course he *did*…

Swimming in the lake of Galilee after all this is for me one of the great experiences, as I bob out in my picture hat. Never mind the water-skiers. Hirsh and H. tell me that they only see a hat floating on the waves. H. feels the same way about his beer as we sit with Hirsh, gazing at the "blue remembered hills" opposite and talking about his life here.

Later the territory remains beautiful – "This way to the Monastery of the Beatitudes" – but we are reminded of the present again because this was the road up which the Israeli Army had to come in '73 to recapture the Golan Heights. Indeed Syria and for that matter Lebanon are beginning to feel near as Hirsh talks of his war experiences.

Suddenly I see "Rosh Pinne". And am aware that this is the kibbutz where Harold's cousin, last glimpsed roughly 30 years ago, actually dwells – Kefar Hanassie the (Anglo-Saxon) kibbutz of the President named for Weizmann. Impulsively we drive there. We wend through driveways with a few young women in shorts pushing babies to a parking lot. There are trees, big ones. It is 1 p.m. We arrive at the dining hall, up shallow steps, glass, swing-doors, a canteen with "Asparagus Hot Pot" chalked up on a board. As H. says, it's like a new university.

We ask rather hesitantly for Moshe Ben Haim, the Hebrew name of H.'s cousin…Suddenly his daughter-in-law is produced. Beverley is a small neat-featured girl with short hair in a red T-shirt and denim shorts. She looks extremely doubtful about everything. It's all rather depressing (I think privately) when we are all at once interrupted by a loud and raucous presence and an unmistakeable American voice.

This is Sophie, Beverley's mother from the Bronx. Sophie, on a visit, is really quite amazing and, as I tell H., if anyone put her on the stage in such a situation, the critics would rightly call it a bit much. For one thing, she instantly makes it quite clear that having worked a lifetime to raise money in the Bronx for the kibbutz, she *loathes* it. And all its works.

Some Sophie-isms: "Everything the kibbutz has, the Bronx has and better". "I couldn't even get my hair done here because I'm not a kibbutz member, and had to go to my cousin in Altamura…"

(This does seem a bit unfair when you think of all the money she has raised. Nevertheless H. says that *he* wouldn't do her hair for her!) "At Passover I wanted to be with my family. What sort of family is 700 people? At home in the Bronx everyone in the family always came to *my* house…"

At this point into this little house, but stocked we notice with stereophonic equipment ("brought from America," says Hirsh), comes Moshe's son Yoni. He is handsome, tall, slim and curly haired. He reacts not so much with sheer side-splitting excitement at Harold's presence (as one *first* might have expected…He has lived in New York for several years) as an odd sort of relief. Later we find out why this is. All the family here having been dreading the arrival of *another* cousin, a much disliked sister's son and their first feeling on seeing Harold is: "It's not him."

But the high point is the meeting with Moshe Ben Haim himself, formerly Morrie Tober, of Hackney. There he is, at the parking lot, back from the local kibbutz council, instantly and recognisably a figure of solid authority. He also incidentally looks rather like Harold's father –

they are first cousins once removed – and has many mannerisms and even ways in common, including the same humorous eyes. To H. he really looks just the same as he did 30 odd years ago when Morrie Tober, as H. puts it, died, and Moshe Ben Haim, an illegal immigrant, was born, to become a father of this kibbutz and with his wife Iris to bear five children. Two while living in a tent. And for 19 years to be shelled constantly from Syria so that among the roses and orange daisies is to be seen a huge shelter built of dark grey stones.

The air-raid shelter.

"These children lived in the trenches," Hirsh tells us.

Moshe has fought – how many wars? He remains a handsome stocky man of 54 years, a thick head of greying hair and that aforesaid authority. He is also a convinced Socialist. His first question to me:

"Do you understand the kibbutz principle?"

Me: "Er, umm."

M. Ben H.: "The kibbutz principle states that the man who negotiates a million pound deal for a kibbutz factory and the man who cleans the basin earn the same amount." Dramatic Pinter pause. "And they are content to do so".

In his house, less well equipped than that of Yoni and Beverley, he reveals further examples of an individual and idealistic character. For example, M. Ben H. to H.: "You've never been here before and I'm sorry you should come here now when we have a Fascist government..."

Also a fine attitude to his relations, most of whom he doesn't speak to, including the aforesaid cousin, his sister's son.

M. Ben H.: "I called a family conference to know if they approved sending him a very strong letter [saying he was not welcome on the kibbutz]. No one supported me except Yoni. But I sent it all the same."

Thus democracy...but there is a twinkle in his eye, as when he talks of Iris, trained at the Tavistock Clinic to give marriage counselling among the young people of the kibbutz, and at the Clinic itself.

"Are they any good? People tell me they are. I don't know. They seem to agree with my wife..."

H. is clearly charmed and moved by the visit,

quite apart from the strange coincidence which has brought us here, from a chance conversation with the allergy doctor, and an unplanned drop-in. I think Moshe too is pleased, tho' he doesn't necessarily let on. But I have the impression that he has boasted to Yoni etc. in the past of Harold.

And I *think* I spy among the paperbacks, at the back, two bright blue Eyre Methuen volumes of his plays.

Yet after all, Moshe is a man who has had a full life in the last 30 years.

Whatever he was doing, he was not exactly waiting for Harold! Indeed he came back from meeting Teddy Sieff and asking him to build a new library.

We drive on to Safat, with a panoramic view of Kefar Hanassie below us and to the Golan Heights. Safat is an interesting but to me faintly odious place, an artists' colony, deliberately so, with signposts this way and that to dozens of *vernissages*. And you can walk through the same *vernissages*, like shops, and see many an oil, all rather garish, of flowers, Jerusalem, and so forth. I don't go for it, tho' it is good to be reminded that these things exist in Israel too and if the pictures had been better, I might not have been so disapproving. What I like best about Safat is the Restaurant Milu, Rumanian, where we eat taramasalata, eat fresh fish and drink white wine, suddenly all three v. hungry. The place has a few tables, a primitive but clean loo. While we are there the sportsmaster of the Bedouin waiter comes to ask for his release for a race because he is such a good runner. The boy has wide eyes, rather African. Outside a film with Henry Fonda is playing.

So over the hills, via a forest planted in memory of the Holocaust, to Haifa and back by the Tel Aviv road. The forest area is like Scotland, Nairn perhaps. My chief memory of the Haifa–Tel Aviv road is of the hoggish Israeli drivers who won't pull over, because by now it's getting late and we are frightened of being late for our dinner party.

Even a panorama of Haifa doesn't really register much, except I think briefly of the immigrant ships in the port in '47. But one thing does register: the wreaths to the dead in the bus incident quite recently, when chiefly the young and innocent died.

We also drive, now in darkness, over the Bab al-Wad and past Latrun, that debatable hilltop of the 1948 war and later. I think of the bus convoys, the pale wounded emerging to greet their relatives at the bus station, a ghastly lottery as to who and what would emerge.

Once at Mishkenot, we both change in ten minutes, how different from our usual need for rests! Israeli spirit. And are taken to a completely different world, that of the Armenian Patriarchate inside the Old City. It's not totally different, because there are police lights flashing and Jackie Kennedy is here. She looks thin and tired, childish almost (says the Patriarch rightly: "You look a child"). But when we meet is sweet as ever.

The scene is so strange, with the Patriarch, an elderly man in a beige cassock, sitting at the top of the room behind a huge desk presiding. He speaks little English and punctuates his remarks with a high shy giggle. But is a poet, a major

Armenian poet, as his Bishop, a beguiling and worldly fellow, explains.

A large television set looks incongruous in the room, with its precious objects in show-cases. Even odder is the banquet in the dining-room (incidentally photographers are snapping us all this time – Armenian photographers I suppose). We have a seated dinner of some splendour, including a whole lamb and red and white wine. But the tablecloth is noticeably dirty and the room even smells a bit. The service is provided by four men, one in an electric blue suit and tie, one a ruffian in a dirty dark suit and an open-neck light green shirt, and two old men in tarbushes.

The Bishop gives a brief clear lecture on the Armenian religion – a national religion essentially, thus no missionaries "and no nuns". Teddy Kollek points out the effect of Israel – that the Greeks now expect to re-take Constantinople.

Bishop: "And the Armenians expect to get back Ararat."

All this gives one a sense again of the extraordinary things the Jews have done in coming here...

We are shown the Armenian Church at night, the many lamps "given by Armenian princesses" flickering. Jackie wows and whispers her way round. The Armenian photographers click the flash in the darkness. Later we two sit on our terrace beneath the filling moon and look at the walls of the Old City and talk.

Later still H. says that it has meant a great deal to him, my being with him in Israel. And later still we fall asleep.

Thursday 18 May

Days rush by, only flaw the heat – but not really because it's part of the experience – and for me my tiresome blotches which have reappeared like Palestinian terrorists, very painful in larger numbers, scotched not killed by the cortisone. I start to take it again, and as a result feel absolutely *ghastly* when Moshe Pearlman takes us to the Knesset, only partially revived by the kindly charm of the burly Clerk of the Knesset. The heat, the distance to walk (security), the raucous schoolchildren coming to have a glimpse of democracy, the little booth of Personal Search Control, all make me feel most faint. But of course there's much of *great* interest here, as ever with Israel, including the fact that they allow in spectators without fear or favour…They took a decision on the subject and decided that democracy must still be seen, even tho' the Knesset is an acknowledged and obvious target of terrorists – the rocket fired last week from near Mount Scopus was probably aimed at the Knesset.

True, the spectator gallery has glass round it. But when you think…We also learn that there is actually an Arab Communist member of the Knesset (five Arab members all told) who congratulated Sadat at the time of the Yom Kippur War.

Clerk (Nathaniel Lorch): "In Britain in the world war would an M.P. who congratulated Hitler on the Battle of Britain be left free?"

The answer is: certainly not. Think of Oswald Mosley imprisoned under 18B.

This Clerk reiterates to us that side of Israel, which for example Paul Johnson feels strongly about, that it has the only democratic assembly in the Middle East, and virtually now in Africa.

Later at Goliath's Bar ("a stone's throw from the King David"), chosen by H. who wants to get back to his culture and hasn't been in this recommended bar, Moshe talks sympathetically about the Socialist side of Israel. Actually H's culture consists of two pushy American girls, one an Amazon of 6' 2" with blonde locks I've seen swimming, and one with short cropped hair who has a line in "Ms Fraser" and signing visitors' books. But we do demolish a litre and a half of Mount Carmel between us, without Moshe who drinks beer. And eat chef's salad. I feel better.

Me to H., looking at very large salad: "You'll need cheese after this."

American Amazon, who enters all our conversations at will from her great height: "We don't have cheese. This is a Kosher restaurant." Moshe reminisces about his coming here, how he had paid his debt to England in the war, his brother killed in Italy, himself having fought, and left free to come here.

Moshe to H.: "You have had an interesting life as a playwright, but when I think of the dull life I would have had in England...here I have believed in and worked for something."

We swim, I read Edmund Wilson, and then are taken to dinner by Felice and Jacoub Malkin at Shamash, a folksy Jewish restaurant. Felice is an artist and Jacoub came here as a boy.

"Shamash" means "sun" and there were large suns on the ceiling. Actually we spend most of our time talking about the Marxist/Communist origins of Zionism (Jacoub was a Marxist) and the fact that there were actually Fascists here before 1940 who wore brown shirts and supported Mussolini. So H.'s cousin was literally right to refer to Begin's government as "Fascist" – anyway in origin. In the late '30s, as a little boy, Jacoub was brought up to defend himself against Jewish Fascists across the road. Also we talk of the revolutionary concept of the Jewish proletarian workers' state to be created for the first time in Israel, essential to Jewish Marxism. Jacoub, himself wounded horribly as a boy on a youth expedition to Masada, was nevertheless thrown out of his kibbutz for wanting to go to University…They needed an accountant.

Jacoub and Felice's apartment is in the German Quarter, opposite a beautiful plain Persian synagogue. A scent of pine in the air from a fire. We drink more Carmel, tea and H. manages to consume a great deal of Scotch – with dire results as we shall see. Felice's pictures abound on the walls, and no one else's.

F.: "I don't allow anyone else on my territory."

Actually I find modern Israeli art crude in rather a horrid way, sort of modern kitsch, in contrast to the personality of Felice which is highly sensitive. I suspect that as Russia produces music and writing, not painting, Israel too will be famous not for its art but of course its music.

Jacoub on Masada: "How did you find it? My own experience was too personal."

It was indeed. On a military expedition aged 15-and-a-half, at 4 a.m. by the camp fire (an area forbidden to Jews) he lost an eye when the illegal grenades at his captain's belt exploded. Eight comrades were killed. Jacoub: "One survivor semaphored, hopelessly, in the direction of the Dead Sea. At the Sea. And a boat did come. All the way to hospital, a British soldier from Intelligence sat by me questioning me, 'what I was doing in the area'."

The Van Leers come round and all talk of their discovery of Israel: "For the first time I do not feel Jewish."

Yet as Felice and Lia agree, they never realised before that all the time in their previous lives they *had* this awareness. Till they came to Israel and lost it. (H. is quite different, as usual. For the first time he really *does* feel Jewish. That's what I suspect and later he confirms it.)

A starry night of great beauty. Bed at 2.00. H. sits up, fatally, mulling.

Friday 19 May

A day much of which is dream-like (but not necessarily in the good sense) and which is the longest day ever known. Starts in Ina Behrs' little French car chugging down the road to Tel Aviv. I have already dashed up to get renewed medicines. H. has a truly appalling hangover. He thus suffers truly appallingly in the back of the car.

Ina, who proves to be of sterling worth in driving us about all day, is really the worst kind of contact for H., being persistent in conversation and vulnerable in personality...

She points out sights merrily, H.'s Israeli bugbear, and when he asks her to go more slowly says uncomprehendingly: "I did not know fast driving gave you a hangover..."

We meet David Samuel at the Weizmann Institute after a journey of which the only other feature is seeing the ruined tanks in the Bal al-Wad, preserved in dark red paint, with memorial stones beside them. David takes in that H. must have a beer, and quickly.

We then go to the Weizmann House, a fascinating '30s place in which for the first time in Israel the style of Simon and Miriam Marks in Ascot and Grosvenor Square etc. is recalled. The colours and sandy wood, off-pale pink, off-pale blue, above all cream. There are high port-holes in the library, where "Chaim and Vera used to play bridge" says Mrs. Yamash, our bossy guide, wife of the Director of the non-scientific side of the Institute. "There is a fire because Vera decided Chaim liked to poke the fire. Look at this portrait of her with a shoulder turned. Very uncharacteristic. She was a cold woman." Later she points out ostentatiously that the Weizmanns slept in separate bedrooms. Indeed she seems to hate Vera Weizmann, enviously, from the grave, insisting on showing her bathroom (shades of Miriam Marks at 47 Grosvenor Square).

"Imagine the luxury of such a bathroom in Israel in the '30s." Later Mrs. Yamash gets H. to sign a programme of *The Homecoming*. "It will be fun." But she does not say for who! And announces before we go that she "will not keep it for very long". She will give it for rubbish.

H.: "For rubbish?" (He's still feeling pretty frightful.)

Mrs. Yamash, firmly: "Rubbish for the soldiers."

I feel, however, something different, pity for her when I learn that she lost her only son in the Yom Kippur War. Of how many people we meet now, nearly all of whom have sons/daughters in the Army, must that be potentially true, that awful phrase, in a couple of years' time...

Lunch is in the cafe dining room of the Institute and H. does winkle out some beer, quite an achievement. I sit next to David's graduate student, Annet, a very pretty if shy girl in a sun-dress with a fine, full bosom – no new Israeli beauty here. She describes her work lucidly – to prove that the effect of drugs such as valium on males and females is quite different because they meet quite different enzymes in their bodies. It seems a good practical task, as opposed to women journalists in England proving that men and women are the same and that women wouldn't need valium if they had better jobs.

Her boyfriend, very attractive but badly (invisibly) burnt in the Yom Kippur War, is an aspirant director who hopes to put on a programme of Israeli-Arab love poetry. Israeli and Arab actors.

"To join us through love," he says humorously. I wish him well. Then we swim in the Wolfsons' private pool, accessed from the house of the Director of the Institute. The Director's wife, Sara Sellar, is one of those ebullient women who might be Italian or Greek or anything Mediterranean. At the pool I see sweet old Sir Isaac Wolfson again, still bumbling along on commercial lines ("I'll sell you twelve tickets for my pool for the price of ten") in his Glaswegian accent. The huge pool reminds me of that from my previous life, the island house in Scotland – tho' much bigger – with its trees and privacy.

On to meet Shimon Peres, Leader of the Opposition. We've managed to avoid seeing anything of the Institute, thank goodness, in the heat and our exhaustion, except people, and a very green impression indeed. This is an oasis. There's a distinct American campus feel too in these official houses.

Shimon Peres lives on the 12th floor of a block overlooking the sea in a suburb of Tel Aviv. A single soldier sits at a desk outside. The view from the apartment is terrific as evening comes, the shutters are opened and a great red sun starts to go down over the sea and the series of great apartment blocks staked out in rows towards it. But the apartment itself, despite some modern art, is that of a middle-class bookish man. It might be in Bonn, for example. Modest, like everything in Israel (except Weizmann's).

Mrs. Peres serves strawberries, cheese, grape-fruit juice, tea on request, and H. is actually offered a Scotch at 5 p.m. (He accepts it at 5.30.)

Also present, the biographer of Ben-Gurion, Shuptai Teket, an immensely talkative man who rather hogs the conversation, albeit interesting-ly, on the subject of Ben-Gurion at first, later on Proust, *No Man's Land*, my books, in fact all our subjects. You know the type. Peres talks less as a result but nevertheless gives the impression of a highly cultured and really well-read man. He is also sensitive and attractive in manner. From the traumatic death of Ben-Gurion's mother, the conversation turns to the greatness of the war-leader in the nation's consciousness which, says Peres, can never be equalled by that of the peace-time leader. Shuptai disagrees vociferously.

Peres: "Yes, but the 'peace-leader' offers nothing but dealing with economic problems…"

We all cite leaders' names feverishly without shaking him. I try Mr. Gladstone but without success. There is some resignation in Peres when he says this, melancholy. I wonder if he is aware in himself of this lack? But he is a well-read man, rushing to Blake's *Life of Disraeli* for the figures of the 1834 franchise when Disraeli was elected – to prove how tiny the power base was – and finding them.

Other topics – Peter Brook and his equation of the theatre and politics which H. denounces. It is an agreeable and civilised interlude, fully justifying George Weidenfeld's description of him in our introduction, as a man he hopes will soon lead Israel again (for his civilised personality). Then Ina comes to fetch us.

H. is enchanted to hear the dialogue which follows:

"Well, Shimon…"

"Ina."

Later, Ina: "We knew each other well once, I worked for Shimon."

Later David Samuel refers to Ina's work too.

H.: "For the Foreign Office?"

David laughs: "That sort of thing. The same line of country."

It is obvious to our excited imaginations that Ina has been a spy!

This is real le Carré country.

We change our clothes at the house of Ina's friends, Ardara Bernstein and husband. She is a novelist, blonde, intense, preoccupied with her children since she is going to New York next day and is seeing-in an au pair. I detect shades of Margaret Drabble, not only in the thin face and blonde hair but in the cleverness. The house is packed with books, many intellectual paperbacks, in this strange seaside resort, Herzelia, where they all live. I can't quite get the measure of it: A "Henry VIII Pub and Restaurant" and professional arty colony. Hanna Maron and Jacoub Rechter's house is, however, lovely, as befits an architect, also full of books, architectural upstairs for him, stage downstairs for her – masses of them, she is evidently most book-oriented. I see everything from Stanislavsky to a *Life of John Gielgud* by Ronald Hayman.

Hanna is delightful, but to me there is something most poignant about her serving dinner, limping round having been seriously injured in a terrorist attack at Munich Airport, with a leg amputated, almost dragging like a partridge, a bird indeed she much resembles. Yet I have to remember she is in two hits and has acted every night for over 300 performances! She has coped. Later we discuss the performer's art versus the loneliness of the writer and she tells me that at the time of her "misfortune" she could never have recovered but for the "sacks" of letters arriving at the Munich Hospital:-

"You have to recover because you have meant this to me."

We also discuss the great difficulty of a husband being married to an actress and she says she has succeeded with Jacoub, after two bosh starts, but by sacrifices – on both sides. Tours not taken abroad, him giving up work and so forth. She gives the impression it has been worthwhile. And indeed Jacoub is so attractive and warm that I think it would be worthwhile! He tells me of the obsession of the younger Israeli generation with the home, always rushing back from the Army on Saturdays. His generation was never like that. Twenty years of war?

The rest of the actors, writers and so forth, while charming are less peculiar to Israel. That is to say Joseph Yadin, a handsome ageing actor, is a common actor's type, as is the young (ish) Israeli actress Ila something or other with long dark hair and bright cat's face, in a white kaftan rather too tight over her bottom. The young playwright Mittelplonkt (can that be right?),

author of *Deep Waters*, and his charming Ondine-
like wife, who directs children's plays, daughter
of the President of the Weizmann Institute, are
also types to be met in London, where they are
shortly going on a Fellowship.

However, our journey back, Ina at the wheel,
is pure Israel – beginning with being totally
lost in this Tel Aviv suburb for hours, and then
stopped at a road block outside Jerusalem for
our passports. Mine is inspected, so is Ina's. H.
doesn't have his and smiles benevolently which
oddly enough seems to be enough.

Bed at 3.00 a.m. It *was* a long day.

Saturday 20 May

I awake early, hot and strained from the previous day. But determined rather grimly to see the Armenian manuscripts evoked so vividly at our dinner.

I'm very glad I did, as I saw another side of Jerusalem – more of an eternal side than the fertile life of Israel, which whatever its origins, is *new*. Not exactly a corrective as another important view.

I was fetched in a large car with an Armenian chauffeur – all the Armenians I have met have been large and handsome and almost brigand-like except for their civilised clothes. The chauffeur was no exception. In the car a smaller dark man with a check shirt.

Me (the usual question): "Where were you born?"

Mr. Hintillian: "Here in Jerusalem."

Me: "Then you have seen many changes in your lifetime."

Mr. H.: "In the Armenian Quarter we do not see changes."

This proves to be the keynote of the visit. Padding through the quiet courtyards of the quarter with the occasional vine, the odd dark-haired rather healthy-looking child playing, the feeling compared to the rest of Jerusalem is utterly, utterly different. I am accompanied by the Archbishop, the liquid-eyed convivial fellow of the dinner party. He tousles the occasional child on its head as he swishes by.

An occasional sign: "Armenian Jerusalem Health Centre" looks incongruous among the stone houses and monasteries, all interlocked, and reminds me that this church is very rich and, according to Peter Halban, criticised for not spending enough on its people...

We reach the library, wooden show-cases within another church (there are seven). The Archbishop reminds me of my idea of Cardinal Manning, the ancient librarian comes out of a historical novel of Harrison Ainsworth – or perhaps from a Verdi opera.

A lifetime of ruthless guarding of treasures. We are joined by an equally picturesque type, Mr. Mondessian (or a name to that effect), everyone's idea of the oily Levantine but not so much oily to be fair as reeking of aftershave. He is fat, with thick dark hair and bulbous eyes, an art dealer:

"I have a wonderful apartment in London, W.2., very near the centre, a lovely house in Paris, a house in Geneva, Switzerland, and a house in Los Angeles...I adore Los Angeles. The people have no taste (the only good collectors are the Jews) but they have such a sense of fun."

Actually he turns out to be a great asset, being knowledgeable and courteous, and a dialogue now breaks out on the subject of these amazing manuscripts. Otherwise I would have been left with the language of Jackie Kennedy, I fear, "Ooh" and "wow". The librarian places down, in turn, four leather-bound volumes, and turning to a page, removes a scrap of coloured silk (new). Something so immediately and strikingly exquisite is revealed (no fumbling in the mind as sometimes happens: "so this is a treasure, but why?") that my pen is not adequate. It's partly the precision of what the artist has done, even the faces are portraits; partly the colour, the use of lapis lazuli, gold, green; partly the use of animals and birds (partridges, peacocks, wood-peckers amongst them); partly the strength of each design, be it the Transfiguration (perhaps the greatest), the Descent into Hell, the Ride into Jerusalem. But one cannot eliminate from one's reaction as one gazes, the sense of the art-ist's *patience*. And this in turn transmutes into reverence. The librarian has found drops of wax, proving the labours went on at night, but we agree that such judgements concerning light today and then are not really relevant.

These illuminations of the Bible were commis-sioned by Armenian princesses and then given to monasteries. They are 12th – 15th century and the preservation is fantastic. There seems no reason now why they should not survive forever – do not ask about the shelling of Jerusalem twice in the last 30 years. What happened to the manu-scripts then? You forget and thus do not ask.

The church/library has a chapel off it for the prince, entirely tiled in blue and white deco-rated tiles, over the arches, in the alcoves, on the floor, everywhere. Another treasure. I think suddenly of the stark Fraser pew in the Eskadale Church.

I am lured by the Archbishop, plus the art dealer and Annie from Mishkenot who has come to fetch me, up to what proves to be an Armenian Old City penthouse. We walk across the roofs, rather like a scene from *On the Waterfront*, Jerusalem version, with birds kept, and a fine view of New Jerusalem. Except when you examine it, most of the buildings are so ugly that it is only the perspective which charms. The Hilton is particularly horrible, built I fear by Jacoub Rechter. However, King David's tower, very close, is at least fine.

The Archbishop's roof garden ("here I sit at night in the cool – and gaze at the Hilton") has snapdragons and Sweet Williams in its pots, I note, as well as Hippeastra.

His library is ornamented with show-cases full of archaeologica.

"I am an amateur archaeologist. Here are my treasures" – much Roman glass.

Me: "A tempting city to live in for a collector."

Archbp: "That is one temptation one does

not pray to God to resist" – said with his usual liquid laugh.

Me, losing my head: "Or as Oscar Wilde said, 'I can resist anything except temptation.'"

This does not go down so well, whether because the Archbishop and the art dealer don't recognise the name of Oscar Wilde or because they do, I'm not sure.

We talk of biography and research; both gents, whether they have heard of Oscar Wilde or not, have heard of and even read Antonia Fraser. I explain the need for time in a biography, for thoughts to mature like wine. Archbishop agrees in terms of his own work.

"I am preparing lectures on Armenian theology for students. This will take me three years."

As I sip white wine ("Please don't disappoint me and ask for juice") I feel I would settle for his life with pleasure, and take *years* over my books.

To lunch at the American Colony Club with the Director of the Jerusalem Theatre, having done some quick shopping for Bedouin kaftans in the Old City, Annie the bargainer. Tiny and smiling, she beats down an enormous Arab from 5001 £S to 240, and I am left with two genuine Bedouin black and striped pink kaftans and an embroidered black and pink jacket. They are old and filthy and God, or rather Allah, knows what they will be used for, but perhaps Flora and I can write mother-and-daughter essays in them? I definitely don't buy one for Harold's son Daniel which had been my plan as I think he would be even more horrified. (Luckily, later, out of the shop, H. thinks mine is pretty, so my eye had not been quite lost in this horrid Arab shop.)

The Director's very tall indeed, 6' 5" or 6' 6". I feel enormous sympathy. He describes his own sufferings as a kibbutz child, through his height.

"I was very tall, I cried when anyone touched me; my mother was divorced, I was the only boy without a daddy in the kibbutz." Awful. However, the lunch has its interest apart from an exciting moment when we learn that Michael

Kustow has arranged for a National Theatre reading here for H. and Peggy Ashcroft. Well *almost* arranged.

The Director is a terrific dove, the most doveish person we have met. He counsels a Palestinian State with Jerusalem as its capital, for example. I think this odd – in Israeli terms – for the Director of the Jerusalem Theatre. Not quite the Kollek spirit? Yet it is only fair to recall that he has been a military correspondent in two wars, and lost a brother in the Yom Kippur War ("Yes, it was lousy"). His much younger girl-friend, a girl with milk-white skin and the most beautiful thick dark auburn hair, is however an example of a very happy kibbutznik – there till she was 16. Now at the University. So it is interesting to find the two types joined up.

The owner of the American Colony is introduced to us, a man of 72, a real Graham Greene figure. Horatio Vesta, who as a boy remembered the Turks leaving, and rolling and re-rolling bandages in the First World War. Now, however, aided by his niece and nephew, young sandy Scottish types from Fife called confusingly Nairn (met by me at Beaufort).

"We knocked about Africa a bit." I suspect them of coming from Rhodesia.

But now heat and strain and meeting people are getting to me. We go back to Mishkenot and I try to rest. Harold of course continues to read that great literary work *O Jerusalem!* avidly. (Later, as evening comes, I persuade him successfully to join me in a rest by taking his spectacles off. So then he couldn't read *OJ!*.)

We go to dinner at Shamash again with Hirsh Goodman and his wife Beulah. Shamash is hot, and I'm still in a state of people-fatigue, tho' the lamb is good. There is another guest whose ebullience is a little irritating.

"Do you know perhaps that play is right? And the old here do want the young to be killed off."

Quite ridiculous – one of the most marked experiences here has been feeling the exact opposite, as I wrote yesterday.

But we are relieved to hear that four Palestinian

terrorists have been shot dead at Orly Airport in Paris – "with precision" says Hirsh ecstatically several times – without managing to spray the innocent tourists of El Al with their machine guns. I remember Harold's similar reaction to the news of the Raid on Entebbe two years ago and the dramatic rescue of the Israeli hostages.

Hirsh goes to the telephone to argue with the censor about his use of the phrase "nuclear war" in an article, as a logical conclusion to present Israeli policy (even H. thinks privately the censor was probably right!).

The evening is much cooler. A short sit under the stars looking at the Old City. Bed – for me – at 11 p.m.

Sunday 21 May

Sunday. "Shabbat," murmurs H. somewhat inaccurately, and makes my breakfast as he does at home.

I potter and gaze at the Old City walls in the afternoon, of what turns out to be quite a fresh if hot day (no more Khamsin and you feel the difference). H. is interviewed for about two hours by the literary editor of the *Jerusalem Post* – one Matthew Nesvisky – in the quiet of the King David bar. I read by the pool, including a paperback life of Begin bought at the hotel bookstore, for as I am buying *My Life* by Golda Meir, I suddenly realise that Begin is the one I don't know about and I can't exercise a boycott over useful knowledge. I'm rewarded not just by a good book (it's by two journalists) which would be too much to ask nor by a blinding revelation proving Begin to be much misunderstood. But by more understanding on my own part. It's as if an ex-head of the Provo IRA became PM of a United Ireland – a cause in which we all believe, but how could one get over the past of brutal violence and murder? One wouldn't. So they don't get over Begin and the Irgun here.

Yet at least one remark of his strikes home: roughly quoted, "Why do they call me a terrorist – not that I mind, I disdain them – and Arafat a guerrilla?" H. finds Nesvisky agreeable and stays some time, although he later has cold feet about an interview of which he cannot see a transcript. "I'm afraid of looseness, he didn't have a tape recorder, he may write loosely, indeed I may have *spoken* loosely…" (These fears show H.'s intuition. The interview was a trite pastiche of what he said.) Understandable fears on the part of H.'s general dislike of looseness, lack of economy I suppose, in language. Yet it is a measure of H.'s serious approach to this place, approval if you like, that he agreed in his mind to give this interview before the man wrote.

In the afternoon I go to the Old City and do some extremely rapid souvenir shopping, finding that the Spirit of Annie is upon me and I can bargain with the best! A Jerusalem ash-tray for Harold's mother, hoping vaguely that the design is neither Islamic nor Catholic. Cotton kaftans – at last – for his son Daniel and my son Benjie, striped and sort of mannish. D. can compose striped and mannish works in Oxford in his, as I see it, and B. don his in the basement pad for entertainment of his schoolfriends (before stripping it off?).

Myself, I favour something pink and white and floating.

It is a lovely late afternoon in the Old City, a light wind, and in the sun which is now golden on the outside walls, I go for a long ramble where Teddy Kollek and the Jerusalem Foundation are making "David's Garden". Everywhere there are stones, paths, new earth, measurements. A notice: "Planted by the Jewish Foundation of Canada". I expect to see Jewish maples, to say nothing of leaves. It is a lovely experience of walking amongst work, especially as by this time, 5 p.m., there are no workers around. I see Mishkenot across the rift and the Montefiore windmill and wave vaguely towards H., in case his "packing" has taken him just to sit on the terrace.

A man follows me and urges me to visit his church. "I am not a guide," he assures me, "but a pleasing person." Like Garbo, but rather pleadingly, I say: "I am one that wants to be by herself." In an obstinate way I absolutely refuse to go into his church although I am rather feeling like going into a church. Doubling back near the Old City, the Catholic wails of Benediction come to me from various quarters. I take my leave of the view of the far-side of the City, wonderful sandy and blue colouring by now.

The whiteish and sandy new houses up the far slopes, making it like a de Staël picture. More tree-planting!

Then I do go into a church, what appears to be an extremely modern and rebuilt one of a

Byzantine nature. There's an over-new feel here, although at the same time it reminds me of Blackfriars at Oxford, with its plainness and a little also of St. Aloysius. I find later it was built by the German Emperor in 1890, a copy of Charlemagne's chapel at Aix-la-Chapelle, which is in turn a copy of Charlemagne's chapel…and so on. Some German nuns, short skirts, short white veils, recite the Hail Mary loudly. I don't feel like saying a prayer myself, but like the idea of this being the Church of the Dormition where traditionally Our Lady lived after the Crucifixion and before her Assumption. As a peaceful old lady's house, one who had witnessed great events, it presents a wonderful view, in short exactly the right sort of situation. A retirement cottage.

I buy some olive wood crosses, small with *Jerusalem* on them, for 3 Israeli £s from a German monk in the church shop. He does not press or bother me and I don't bargain with him. They are for my Catholic friends, which may include such varied people as my mother, my sister Rachel, my children (some) and perhaps, who knows, Hugh, who received many such objects from *his* mother, once my fearsome mother-in-law and a passionate Catholic; he might, I feel, like the tradition continued.

I walk past the elegant monastery, walk down, slithering over new earth and ill-placed stones, then up to Mishkenot. Through the window, H. preparing for a shower looks rather like a Japanese wrestler.

Later we sit outside on a perfect evening as a full moon is gradually defined in the sky, and the shimmering sea-like effect of the desert beyond is lost. In the end the moon is very strong indeed. But the walls do not lose their own strength. When Peter Halban brings us the Mishkenot Visitors' Book, I am as a result moved to make some allusion to Napoleon at the Pyramids, to the French soldiers, and centuries of history looking down. For I do feel that these clean bright old walls are looking at me and have done so for two weeks.

But H. writes with simplicity: "Thank you! Wonderful".

We both note other contributions, such as a pretentious meander from John Vaizey (signed typically "Vaizey of Greenwich") about interpreting Israel to the world. The signatures of Nathalie Sarraute, Irwin Shaw, and musicians.

***

The evening at David and Dorothy Harman's is quite American in flavour, the deposition of the buffet, long drinking-time. Many of the guests are American and I myself am not convinced the Harmans will in the end settle here. They're such a Cambridge, Mass., young couple! And Dorothy already fears Israeli aggression acting on her five-year-old son, quite apart from Arab aggression. David explains the terrible rift in Israeli education between secular and religious (70%:30%) which makes a great division until the Army is reached. By then it's unhealable. Will he stay?

Antonia Fraser

But H. and I agree they are bright and sympathetic. The *New York Times* local man in the meantime tells us a horror story about the infamous town of Nablus where, with his children and Israeli neighbour in the back of a station wagon, he was stoned, all glass broken, surrounded by the mob.

In the end it was an Arab who, for whatever motives, led him to safety...The visit was just after the imposition of V.A.T. – all the same, this seems to complete our picture of the dreaded Nablus. Tony Lewis, of all people, is there, at the end of a tour of the Middle East for the *N.Y. Times*. H. elects to be very irritated by him and later booms on regarding his voice ("the voice of the expert") in a late-night snarl! I actually find it very interesting to encounter "an expert" or if not that, someone who has actually been to these fated Arab countries *now*, interviewed Sadat a few days ago – an interview incidentally which, plus the Israeli disregard of it, obsessed H. at the time.

Like the *Times* leader I suddenly read, arising out of this very interview, called *Sadat and the West Bank*, written in such completely different spirit, Tony Lewis reminded me how incredibly cut off Israel is. It's a cut-off society. Tony L.: "The Israelis are *so irritating*! They are so wonderful, but they're so irritating that they can't understand how others see them. They won't even listen." (He's Jewish of course so he can say this, East Coast Jewish, if there is such a thing. There *is*. Because that's what H. dislikes about him, I decide in the end late at night.)

Actually it is what one feels – except I don't find them irritating myself, just wonderful. But then I have not interviewed Begin, have I? Nor argued about Judea and Samaria with him. Tony tells me of Begin in Washington relentlessly holding up proceedings by always referring to "J and S" which is always corrected by the Americans to "the West Bank". So no one gets anywhere. The next day the Americans let it go, purely to get on with the talks, which are after all very important.

Begin, in triumph: "So you see, our arguments wore them down."

Monday 22 May

5 a.m. call. But it's a lovely day and the sun comes sharply through the window of the Church of the Dormition like a red theatre neon light. We drink coffee outside on the terrace, and I pick a geranium from the new Kollek plantings for this Diary. It should really be a piece of honeysuckle but I haven't the energy to scuttle that far in my pink-and-white check robe.

H.: "We should always get up at five in the morning." He speaks with great conviction in his black-and-white dressing-gown.

We leave Mishkenot, driven by the only good driver we have had in Israel, as H. accurately points out. A mist surrounds us as we pass beyond Jerusalem. The Knesset peers over its tree protection, like some ridiculous wendy-house or perhaps it's worried about an Arab attack? On the road, H. holds my hand, but mainly recalls Ina's driving, her triumphs and her dialogues.

At the airport the *Jerusalem Post* tells us the S. Lebanese terrorists have vowed to make further "successful", as they put it, attempts. The security is fantastic, including a personal interrogation, before you check-in the luggage, by a polite young Israeli woman security officer in slacks and jersey. She has short hair and is a new Israeli, but not a new Israeli beauty. She asks us searching questions about relations here and even about Teddy Kollek, having read his letter of invitation carefully.

She asks us, looking at our passports: "What is your relationship to each other?" Harold, expansively with what I feel is an Anew McMaster gesture: "We're lovers!"

Girl, rather shyly: "I'm sorry…"

Glimpse of new Israeli Puritanism. After all, we're not Puritans. But I do feel a bit like Aunt Violet Powell for a moment, quite the English lady. All this un-English fuss!

"No, I am *not* Jewish, and thus I do not have any relations here."

Voices rise round us, including a desperate American brayer: "Rabbi – we can't board, we haven't got boarding-passes."

Rabbis, mainly plump and young and WASP-looking, are indeed in abundance. Once in the inner circle, searched in cubicles (actually I'm not but H. takes much longer and I think is) we relax. I stop trying to spot a) the terrorists b) the Israeli cops, in the cast of this disaster movie.

H. buys me an enormous pair of Israeli agate earrings at the jewellery counter. "I am in a position to buy you something." He gives his name for the bill.

"Just like the writer," comments the lady behind the counter with interest, "including the spelling."